Getting Started

This book is filled with fun, easy-to-make crafts, and each one begins with a paper bag. You'll find a wide variety of things to make, including toys, games, and gifts.

Directions

Before you start each craft, read the directions and look closely at the photograph, but remember—it's up to you to make the craft your own. If we decorate a craft with markers, but you want to use glitter paint and stickers, go for it. Feel free to stray from our directions and invent new crafts.

Work Area

It's a good idea to keep your work area covered. Old newspapers, brown paper (yet another use for grocery bags!), or old sheets work well. Also, protect your clothes by wearing a smock. A big, old shirt does the job and gives you room to move. Finally, remember to clean up when you've finished.

Materials

You'll need a lot of paper bags, so start saving now. Ask friends and relatives to help. Keep your craft-making supplies together, and before making each craft, check the "You Will Need" list to make sure you have everything. In this list, we'll often specify which type of paper bag we used. For most crafts, however, any type of paper bag will work. When selecting a bag, think about what size you want your finished craft to be.

Other Stuff

When we show several similar crafts, we'll often list numbered directions that apply to all of the crafts, then specific directions for each craft.

Here's a painting tip: Sometimes department-store bags have a shiny coating, and poster paint won't stick to them. Try mixing liquid soap with the paint. It takes longer to dry, but it works. Acrylic paints also work.

That's about all. So, find a bunch of paper bags, select a craft that you like, and have some fun. Before you know it, you'll be showing everyone what you made with paper bags.

Bag Animal Bonanza

Gather bags of all sizes, and use your creativity to turn them into friendly beasts.

You Will Need:

- paper bags
- pencil
- scissors
- thin cardboard
- glue
- markers
- construction paper
- paints
- chenille sticks
- pompons
- newspaper
- boxes
- masking tape
- yarn
- feathers
- wiggle eyes

To Make the Animals on This Page

1 Turn the bag upside down. Use a pencil to draw the animal shape, using the corner folds as legs. Draw a head on one side and a tail on the other side of the bag. Cut out the animal.

2 Cut a piece of cardboard to fit inside each leg, and fold it lengthwise so it matches the fold in the leg. Glue each piece of cardboard in place to strengthen the legs.

To Make the Giraffe

Fold the neck up and glue it in place. Draw spots and other details on the body with markers. Glue on a mane cut from construction paper.

To Make the Skunk

Paint the skunk. Let it dry. Using a pencil, poke a few holes in a line along the center of the tail, and weave a chenille stick through them. Shape the tail as you wish. Glue on a pompon as a nose.

To Make the Turtle

For the turtle's shell, cut out a piece of construction paper and decorate it with markers. Glue it on. Draw a face with markers.

Look What You Can Make With

Paper Bags

Edited by Judy Burke
Photographs by Hank Schneider

Boyds Mills Press

Craft Coordinator:

Carrie Abel

Contributors:

Sharon Addy
Caroline Arnold
Jenny Bak
Laura G. Beer
Anne Bell
Doris Boutin
Marie E. Cecchini
Diane Cherkerzian
Nancy Dunlea
Gladys Emerson
Julie Fultz
Mavis Grant

Edna Harrington
Carmen Horn
Ellen Javernick
Janet Kent
Garnett Kooker
Kathleen Peelen Krebs
Karen Kremsreiter
Twilla Lamm
Ruth Everding Libbey
Lee Lindeman
Doreen Macklen
Clare Mishica

June Rose Mobly
James W. Perrin, Jr.
Luella Pierce
Simone Quick
Necia Sneed Ramsey
Kathy Ross
Mary Jo Rulnick
Beth Stevens
Sharon Dunn Umnik
Lynn Wasnak
Linda Weissinger
Doris Woodliff

Copyright © 1999 by Boyds Mills Press
All rights reserved

Published by Bell Books
Boyds Mills Press, Inc.
A Highlights Company
815 Church Street
Honesdale, Pennsylvania 18431
Printed in the United States of America

Publisher Cataloging-in-Publication Data
Burke, Judy, editor.
    Look what you can make with paper bags : over ninety pictured crafts and dozens of other ideas /
edited by Judy Burke ; photographs by Hank Schneider.—1st edition
[48]p. : col. ill. ; cm.
Summary: Toys, games, and other ideas all from paper bags.
ISBN 1-56397-717-6
1. Handicraft—Juvenile literature. 2. Paper bags—Juvenile literature.
[1. Handicraft. 2. Paper bags.] I. Schneider, Hank, ill. II. Title.
745.54—dc21   1999   CIP
Library of Congress Catalog Card Number 97-77904

First edition, 1999
Books in this series originally designed by Lorianne Siomades
The text of this book is set in 10pt Avant Garde Demi, titles 43pt Gill Sans Extra Bold

10 9 8 7 6 5 4 3 2 1

Start with the creatures shown here, then see what others you can make.

To Make the Animals on This Page

1 For the head, stuff a bag half full with newspaper.

2 For the body, glue paper over a box.

3 Cut out legs, wings, or ears from cardboard.

To Make the Tiger

Glue the bag closed. Glue it on the end of the body, with the bottom of the bag as the face. Glue on cardboard ears and legs. Paint the tiger. Use markers to add stripes. Glue on a chenille-stick tail and whiskers, a pompon nose, and eyes cut from paper.

To Make the Bird

Fold the end of the bag to form a beak. Glue it to secure it. Glue the head on top of the body. Glue on cardboard wings and legs. Paint the bird. Add a feathery tail and wiggle eyes.

To Make the Elephant

Twist the end of the bag into a trunk. Wrap it with masking tape. Glue the head on the end of the body. Glue on cardboard ears and legs. Paint the elephant. Add a braided yarn tail and a yarn mouth. Draw eyes and other details with markers.

More Ideas

Try to think of other ways a bag can be used to make an animal. You might stuff a bag with newspaper to create a body, and glue on paper features.

Make a habitat for your animals. Create trees, ponds, flowers, and other features from paper bags.

Broom Friend

Dance together, or just keep each other company.

You Will Need:

- grocery bag
- paints
- broom
- newspaper
- string
- scissors
- construction paper
- glue
- pencil
- accessories

1 For the head, turn the bag upside down and paint a face on one side.

2 Wrap the broom with newspaper. Place it in the bag. Add more newspaper to fill out the head. Tie the bag closed.

3 For hair, glue on strips cut from construction paper. Curl the ends around a pencil. Add an old hat and a scarf for decoration.

More Ideas

Create several broom characters and put on a play.

Make a hobbyhorse by creating a horse's head from a bag and attaching it to a broom.

Body Drawing

Personalize a wall hanging with pictures of your favorite things.

You Will Need:

- grocery bags
- scissors
- tape
- pencil
- old magazines
- glue

1 Cut open the bags. Tape the ends together to make a piece of paper that is a little longer and wider than yourself. Lie down on the paper, and ask a friend to trace around you with a pencil. Cut out the shape.

2 Cut out pictures of things you like from magazines. Glue them to the shape. Hang up your body drawing.

More Ideas

Create a jumbo paper doll and clothes. Attach the clothes to the doll with self-adhesive Velcro pieces.

Magnificent Mobiles

Decorate for a party or spice up your room with these colorful mobiles.

You Will Need:

- grocery bags
- paints
- glue
- scissors
- construction paper
- newspaper
- stapler
- crepe paper
- reinforcement rings
- yarn and thread
- tape
- pinecones

1 Turn a bag upside down. On one side, paint a face or glue on cut-paper features. Stuff the bag with newspaper. Staple the bag closed. Glue the end down.

2 Poke two holes an inch apart on top of the head. Add reinforcement rings to the holes so the paper doesn't rip. Tie a long piece of yarn through the holes for a hanger.

To Make the Witch

For hair, glue on crepe paper. Tie a knot about two inches above the head. Cut a circle from construction paper for the brim of the hat. Make a hole in the center, and pull the yarn through, letting the brim rest on the knot. To make the top of the hat, roll a piece of paper into a cone shape. Thread the yarn through the hat and tape the top of the hat to the brim. Glue on yarn as a hatband.

To Make the Owl

Poke two holes on each side of the bottom of the bag. Tie a long piece of thread through each set of holes. A few inches from the owl's body, wrap each piece of thread around an upside-down pinecone. Wrap another pinecone below. Glue cut-paper features on the pinecones so they look like little owls. Glue cut-paper wings on the sides of the large owl.

More Ideas

Design a mobile to match a party theme. If it's a Fourth of July party, paint the American flag on a bag, and hang mini stars and streamers from it. If it's a birthday party, paint a cake on a bag, and hang tiny wrapped boxes from it as presents.

Make a wind-chime mobile by decorating the main bag festively and hanging jingle bells, cans, or other noisy objects from it. Hang it where there's a breeze.

Rustic Log Cabin

You're the architect! Design a house, roll up some paper logs, and create a log cabin.

You Will Need:

- grocery bags
- corrugated cardboard
- scissors
- bakery box with a plastic window
- markers
- tape and glue
- pencil
- plastic drinking straws
- paints
- sand

1 From cardboard, draw and cut out four walls with tabs. Each wall should have two tabs, one at the top of the left side and one at the bottom of the left side. Cut holes in the walls for windows and doors.

2 To make windows, cut squares from the window of a bakery box. Use a marker to draw panes. Tape the windows behind the cut-out window holes on the walls.

3 Put glue on the front of the tabs, and assemble the walls, with the tabs inside the cabin. To make each "log," cut a strip from a paper bag, roll it around a pencil, and glue the edges. Glue the logs on the walls. Let the end of every second log stick out to interlock with the logs from the other walls, as shown in the photo.

Then make a woodland setting, complete with a lake and trees.

4 From cardboard, cut out a roof to fit the cabin. Glue it on. Make a chimney from cardboard. Cut the bottom to fit the angle of the roof. Glue it on. Glue the cabin on a piece of cardboard. Add details with a marker. Add a porch roof and other details with cardboard and paper rolls.

To Make the Trees

Cut a long, 3-inch-wide strip from a bag. Draw a line diagonally across it. Cut fringe on one side of the line. Starting with the end with the short fringe, wrap the strip around a plastic straw, gluing it and bending out the fringe as you go. Tape down the end. Cut a square from cardboard and cut a slit in the middle. Insert the straw end through the slit, cut the end in half vertically, and tape the two straw parts to the cardboard.

To Make the Lake

Cut out a lake shape from a paper bag. Paint it, leaving the beach section unpainted. Spread glue on the beach section and sprinkle sand on it. Let it dry. Create a dock by gluing paper logs onto a piece of cardboard.

More Ideas

Adapt the rolled-paper technique to add a 3-D effect to other crafts. Decorate a photo frame or a pencil can to look wooden by gluing on rolled paper-bag strips.

Breeze Catchers

With the help of some string and a little creativity, send those bags soaring into the blue.

You Will Need:

- long bags
- grocery bags
- markers
- scissors
- construction paper
- foil
- stapler
- fabric
- hole punch
- reinforcement rings
- string
- glue
- crepe paper
- paints

1 Follow the directions for the kite you want to make.

2 Punch two holes near the open end of the bag. Add reinforcement rings to the holes so the paper doesn't rip. Tie a long piece of string through the holes and knot it.

3 To fly your kite, hold it by the string and run in the wind.

More Ideas

Create your own kite designs. Try an airplane, a hot-air balloon, or an eagle.

To Make the Streamer Kite

Fold over the top edge of a grocery bag to form a cuff. Glue crepe paper under the cuff and near the bottom of the bag.

To Make the Fish Kite

Use markers and cut paper to create a face at the open end of a long bag. Glue on scales cut from construction paper and foil. Staple on a knotted fabric tail.

To Make the Nautical Wind Sock

Paint nautical flag symbols on a long bag. Punch two holes at the closed end, glue on reinforcement rings, and tie a long string through each hole. Cut out paper rectangles and paint them. Fold them in half around the strings, and glue them in place.

Winter Warm-Up Bag

This is the perfect gift on a wintry day: a decorative bag filled with delicious hot-cocoa mix.

You Will Need:

- lunch bag
- white paper
- scissors
- glue
- glitter
- 2 cups instant dry milk
- 1 cup sugar
- ½ cup unsweetened cocoa
- plastic sandwich bag that zips
- ink pen
- ribbon

1 To decorate the bag, fold a square piece of paper several times. Cut out triangles and other shapes from the edges. Open the paper, and glue it on the bag. Add glue-and-glitter decorations.

2 Mix together the dry milk, sugar, and cocoa. Put the mixture in the sandwich bag. Write the following directions on a piece of paper:

Place three heaping teaspoons in a cup,
Add boiling water, stir, and drink it up!

3 Put the sealed sandwich bag and the directions in the decorated bag. Tie it closed with ribbon, and give it as a gift.

More Ideas

Decorate the bag for any occasion. In the summer, use iced-tea or lemonade mix instead of hot cocoa.

Basket of Flowers

Ring in spring with this bright bouquet.

You Will Need:

- grocery bags
- compass
- pencil
- scissors
- glue
- markers
- construction paper
- yarn

1 Cut open the bags. Use a compass to draw two large circles of equal size. Cut them out. Cut one circle in half. Glue the curved edge of one half onto the other circle, forming a pocket. Use markers to decorate it.

2 Cut flowers from construction paper. Place them in the basket. Make a hole in the top of the basket. Tie yarn through the hole as a hanger.

More Ideas

On the back of each flower, write a chore that you're willing to do, and give the bouquet as a gift.

Make an autumn decoration by cutting out paper vegetables instead of flowers.

Wear It on Your Head!

Throw on one of these wacky hats, and see how many smiles you get. You can also use these hats as starting points for some unique costumes.

You Will Need:

- grocery bags
- white bags
- ruler
- scissors
- stapler
- construction paper
- chenille stick
- pencil
- glue
- markers
- hole punch
- yarn
- cotton balls
- ribbon
- paints
- plastic wrap
- cardboard tubes

To Make the Spaceman Mask

Put a grocery bag over your head. Place your hand on the bag where it covers your face. Remove the bag, leaving your hand on that spot. Draw an oval-shaped window where your hand was, then cut out the window. Glue a piece of plastic wrap over the window. Cut a hole in the bag below the window. Decorate the mask with markers.

For antennae, curl the ends of a chenille stick around a pencil. Fold it in half and staple it to the top of the mask. For each "ear," snip slits around one end of a short cardboard tube. Cut a matching hole in each side of the mask. Insert the tubes, slit end first, then flatten the slits against the inside of the mask and glue them in place. On each side of the mask, cut out a U-shaped piece at the bottom so the mask can fit comfortably on your shoulders.

To Make the Colonial Wig

Cut a grocery bag in the shape of a wig with a ponytail in the back. Spread glue over a section of the wig, and press cotton balls onto it. Continue until the entire wig is covered. Let it dry. Tie a ribbon in a bow around the ponytail.

To Make the Rabbit or Donkey Ears

Use a paper bag that will fit on your head. Cut the bag so it's about 6 inches long. Fold the open end up 2 inches all around, then fold it once again. For the ears, cut two triangular pieces from a bag. Fold the bottom corners inward, and glue them in place. Glue the ears into the fold of the hat. Decorate the ears with paints or markers. Add ribbon ties.

To Make the Eagle Hat

Find a white bag that will fit on your head. Cut one of the narrow sides down the middle to the bottom of the bag, then cut straight across the bottom. Fold in the resulting flaps and glue them down. Fold the opposite corner inside. Glue this down.

From construction paper, cut out two sides of a beak. Glue them together along the top end. Glue the beak to the hat, and glue the top of the hat closed. Let it dry. Use a marker to draw eyes. Fold up the bottom of the bag for strength, then punch holes along this border. Lace yarn ties through the holes.

To Make the Mouse Hat

Cut out a 9-inch square from a grocery bag. Fold it into a triangle. For the band, cut an 11 1/2-inch-by-1 1/2-inch strip from the bag. Staple the band to the corners opposite the fold. Glue on cut-paper ears, eyes, and a nose. For the tail, staple on a chenille stick and curl it around a pencil.

More Ideas

To make a bonnet, make a larger version of the doll's hat on page 33. To make a long-hair wig, find a brown bag that fits on your head, then cut long fringe in the sides and back of it. Try these: cowboy hats, berets, sailor caps, or sun hats.

Gift Stocking

Make a personalized stocking to hang by the chimney with care.

You Will Need:

- grocery bag
- scissors
- hole punch
- yarn
- construction paper
- markers
- glue

1 Cut two stocking shapes of equal size from a bag. Hold them together and punch holes around the edges, about an inch apart. Lace them together with yarn, and make a loop at the end.

2 From construction paper, cut out a cuff and snowman. Decorate them with markers and glue them on.

More Ideas

Make a stocking card. Cut out two stocking shapes and lace them together on the long straight side. Decorate the front of the card, and write a message inside.

Make a stocking for your pet, and fill it with treats and toys.

Hanukkah Banner

Use this banner as a decoration or as a fire-safe menorah. The "flames" are removable.

You Will Need:

- grocery bag
- scissors
- yarn
- glue
- pencil
- glitter
- tissue paper
- markers

1 Cut open a bag, and cut out a large rectangle for the banner. Lay a long piece of yarn along the top. Fold the paper over it, then glue it in place. Tie the yarn ends together to form a hanger. Use a pencil to draw a menorah on the banner. Go over these lines with glue, then add glitter. Let it dry.

2 For each candle, roll a square piece of paper bag into a tube. Add glue, then place them on the banner. Make "flames" by inserting tissue-paper pieces into the candles. Use markers to write "Happy Hanukkah" on the banner.

More Ideas

Make a birthday banner with a paper cake and candles (as in step 2). Add things that are special to the person whose birthday it is.

Wreaths for All Seasons

Twist, curl, or mold a bag into a festive wreath for any occasion.

You Will Need:

- grocery bags
- scissors
- tape
- yarn or twine
- pinecones, dried flowers, and sticks
- ruler
- gift wrap
- glue
- ribbon
- paper plate
- pencil
- construction paper

To Make the Curly Wreath

Cut out the center of a paper plate. Use the donut shape as the base for your wreath. Cut 7-inch-by-3-inch pieces from a paper bag. At both short ends of each piece, cut fringe 3 inches deep. Curl the fringe around a pencil, then glue the uncut parts onto the base. When the base is covered, crush small pieces of construction paper into balls and glue them on. Add a paper bow. Tie on a twine hanger.

To Make the Pinecone Wreath

Cut a paper bag down one side, and cut off the bottom section. Roll the paper into a tube, crumpling it as you go. Shape the rolled paper into a circle. Tape the ends together. Decorate the wreath with yarn, and tie on pinecones, dried flowers, and sticks. Add a yarn loop as a hanger.

To Make the Tiny Wreath

Cut a 3-inch-by-36-inch strip of paper from a grocery bag. Crush and twist the strip tightly together so it looks like a rope. Shape it into a circle. Tape the ends together. Cut out hearts from gift wrap, and glue them on. Tie on a ribbon bow.

More Ideas

Make a wreath for any season. Tie on flowers, toy birds, and ribbons for spring. Add seashells, sandpaper castles, and paper suns for summer. Glue on nuts, leaves, and pinecones for autumn. Add cotton-ball snowmen, foil ice-skates, and ice-cream-stick skis for winter.

Paper-Bag Party!

It doesn't take much to throw together a party that's fun and inexpensive. Just grab some bags and make your own games, toys, and decorations.

You Will Need:

- paper bags
- markers
- stickers
- streamers
- glue
- scissors
- construction paper
- string
- treats and small toys
- newspaper
- stapler
- plastic film canisters
- dried beans
- pencils
- tape

To Make the Lantern Decorations

For each decoration, cut down the back seam of a lunch bag and cut off the bottom to get a large rectangle. Decorate it with markers, then fold it lengthwise. Cut slits on the fold about an inch apart. Open it up, and glue the short ends together. Cut a strip from another bag as a handle and glue it on. Set it on the table or hang it up.

To Make the Place Mats

For each place mat, cut off one large side from a grocery bag. Cut the edges in a wavy pattern. Decorate it with markers.

To Make the Piñata

The bottom of a bag will be the top of the piñata. Use markers, stickers, streamers, and cut paper to decorate it. Leave 3 inches by the open end blank. At the top of the piñata, poke two holes on opposite sides. Thread a 3-foot-long string through one hole and out the other. Knot the ends together. Fill the piñata with treats and small toys. Use old newspaper as filler. Close the open end of the piñata, fold it down, and staple it closed.

How to Play

With an adult's permission, hang your piñata, have someone blindfold you, and swing at the piñata with a plastic bat. Take turns with others until the piñata breaks. Share the treats and toys.

To Make the Maracas

For each maraca, decorate a lunch bag with markers. Fill a film canister halfway with dried beans, and put on the lid. Wrap it in a piece of newspaper and put it in the bag. Stuff the bag halfway with newspaper. To make a handle, stick a pencil in the middle of the newspaper, and gather the bag opening around it. Wrap the handle with tape to secure it.

More Ideas

Make a gift bag for each guest as a party favor. See pages 20 and 21 for ideas.

Play a mystery-bag game. Place different objects in lunch bags. Have the guests feel the objects and try to guess what they are.

17

Autumn Scarecrow

This fellow is too friendly to scare away crows, but he'll look great as an indoor autumn decoration.

You Will Need:

- paper bags
- scissors
- newspaper
- stapler
- tape
- twine
- construction paper
- straw hat
- bandanna

1 For the body, turn a bag upside down. Poke a hole in each side near the top for arm holes. For arms, roll newspaper into a tube, and push it through the holes. Stuff the body with crumpled newspaper, then fold and staple the open end shut.

2 For the head, stuff a smaller bag with newspaper. Twist and tape the bag closed to form a neck. Make a hole in the top of the body, and insert the neck. Tape it in place.

3 Roll newspaper for legs. Staple brown paper around them, leaving some newspaper sticking out at the bottom. Staple the legs to the body.

4 Tie twine near the ends of the arms and legs, then cut fringe in the newspaper. Glue cut-paper patches and facial features on the scarecrow. Add a straw hat and a bandanna.

More Ideas

To turn your scarecrow into a backpack, don't stuff the body with newspaper. Cut around the top part of the body to form an opening, and add two ribbon straps to the back.

Make a floppy shelf doll with fabric legs. When you set it on a shelf, the legs will hang loosely over the edge.

Souvenir Trunk

This is the perfect container for treasures—letters, movie stubs, invitations, and other keepsakes.

You Will Need:

- grocery bag
- scissors
- glue
- shoe box and lid
- tissue paper
- ribbon
- gold gift wrap

1 Cut open the bag, and glue the paper on the outside of the shoe box and lid. Glue tissue paper inside them.

2 Put the lid on the box. To make straps, glue two pieces of ribbon around the box. Start at the front of the lid, and end at the front of the box.

3 Cut out a latch and other details from gold gift wrap. Glue them on.

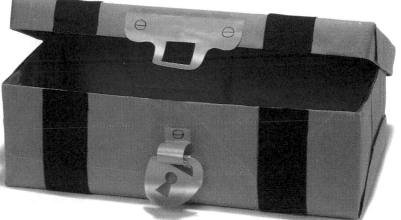

More Ideas

Decorate a clothes storage box to match the season when the stored clothes are worn.

Decorate the outside of a stationery box with used stamps, maps, and postcards. Create stationery and envelopes to put inside.

A Journal Just for You

Create poems and stories, write about your adventures, or jot down the day's events in this leather-like journal.

You Will Need:

- paper bag
- glue
- blank notebook
- soft cloth
- brown cream shoe polish
- markers

1 Rip a bag into pieces, and glue them over the entire cover of the notebook.

2 Using the cloth, rub a little shoe polish smoothly over the cover. Let it dry.

3 Cut out a rectangle from another bag. Fold in the sides to form a frame. Glue it on the cover, and add polish. Write "Journal" with markers.

More Ideas

Make a travel journal. On the cover, glue pictures of wherever you're going. Inside, write about what you see on your trip.

Decorative Gift Bags

Spice up a plain old brown bag and transform it into a handsome gift holder.

You Will Need:

- paper bags
- construction paper
- glue
- pencil
- scissors
- ribbon
- markers
- tissue paper
- old greeting card
- paper doily
- glitter
- hole punch
- string
- blunt table knife
- potato
- paints
- pompon

To Make the Reindeer Bag

Fold down the top 4 inches of a bag to form a flap. From construction paper, cut out antlers, a bow tie, a tongue, eyes, and eyelashes. Curl the eyelashes around a pencil. Glue the antlers near the fold of the flap, glue the eyes, eyelashes, and tongue on the flap, and glue the bow tie below the flap. Add a pompon as a nose.

To Make the Lion Bag

From construction paper, draw and cut out the front view and the back view of a lion. Glue them onto the front and back of a shopping bag with handles. Add details with markers.

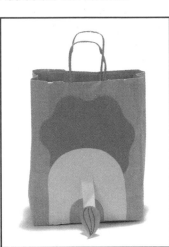

To Make the Happy-Lady Bag

Fold down the top 3 inches of a bag to form a flap. On one piece of paper, draw and color a person's head with a hat and collar, then cut it out. On another piece of paper, draw and color a person's body, then cut it out. Glue the head part on the flap. On the bag under the flap, glue the body. Under the neck, poke two holes through the flap and the bag. Thread ribbon through the holes and tie a bow. This will hold the bag closed.

Use your creativity, and people will admire the bag as much as the gift inside!

To Make the Bag for Mom or Dad

Cut out a picture from an old greeting card. Glue it onto a paper doily, then glue both of them onto a paper bag. Use markers, glue, and glitter to decorate and write a message on the bag. Place a gift inside. Fold in the bag's opening about 1 inch. Close the bag and punch holes across the top. Lace string through the holes and tie the bag closed.

To Make the Birthday Bag

Glue construction paper onto the wide sides of a grocery bag, from the bottom to as high as you want the handles. With a pencil, draw a line around the bag a few inches below the top of the construction paper. Draw a handle on each wide side. Cut off the top of the bag, cutting around the handles. Then cut out the insides of the handles. Decorate the bag with ribbon and markers. Place some tissue paper in the bag.

To Make the Star-Print Bag

Cut a potato in half. With an adult's help, use a table knife to carve an upraised moon shape on one half and an upraised star shape on the other half. Press the potato halves into poster paint, then press them onto a bag to make star prints and moon prints. Let the paint dry. Put a gift in the bag. Fold over the top of the bag, and punch holes through the flap. Lace yarn through the holes, and tie it.

More Ideas

Weave your own gift bag by cutting wide strips in a bag from the opening to the bottom, then weaving strips cut from another colored bag horizontally through the bag strips. Glue or tape the ends in place, and glue on paper handles.

Cover a paper shopping bag with scrap-fabric patches, or glue brightly colored yarn around it.

Autograph Hound

This pooch is perfect for displaying all of your friends' signatures.

1 Cut out a large rectangle from the grocery bag. Fold it accordion-style.

2 Open the paper. Use markers to draw a dog across the whole piece of paper.

3 Have your friends sign the card at the end of the school year. Keep it as a memento.

You Will Need:

- grocery bag
- scissors
- markers

More Ideas

Use the autograph hound as a get-well card from a group of people.

Make a similar card using another long animal, such as a giraffe, lizard, otter, or snake.

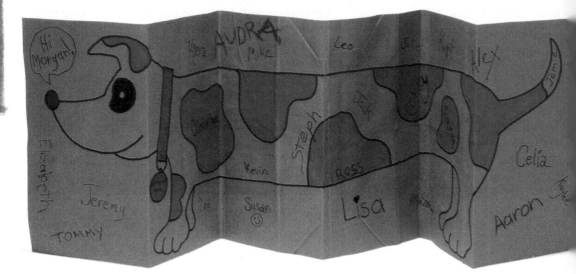

Toadstool Pencil Holder

Is there mush-room for pencils in this holder? There certainly is!

You Will Need:

- lunch bag
- rubber band
- paints

1 To form the cap of the toadstool, carefully turn the open end of the bag so that a few inches of it hang over the sides.

2 Put a rubber band around the section beneath the cap.

3 Paint the toadstool, and let it dry. Put your pencils, pens, and markers in it.

More Ideas

For a puppet-show set, make palm trees by cutting palm fronds from the folded part of the bag.

Invent your own funny creature by cutting hair from the folded part and painting on a face.

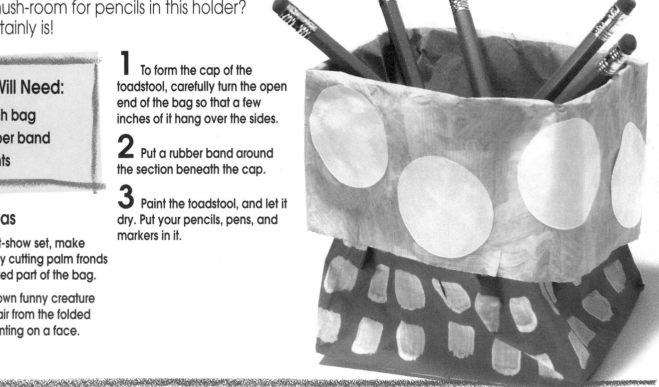

Strings of Bag Beads

Roll them, twist them, or bend them. Then string them up and wear them!

You Will Need:

- grocery bags
- scissors
- markers, glitter, or paints
- glue
- toothpick
- hole punch
- yarn or string

To Make a Tube Bead

Cut a long strip from a grocery bag. Make it as wide as you'd like your bead. Use markers, glitter, or paints to decorate a few inches at one end of it. Then, starting at the plain end, roll the strip around a toothpick. Glue down the end.

To Make the Accordion-Style Bead

Cut a strip from a bag. Decorate it on both sides with markers or paints, then fold it accordion-style. Punch a hole in each section between the folds.

To Make a Necklace, Bracelet, or Anklet

Create as many beads as you like, then arrange them on your work space. Wrap tape around the end of a length of string or yarn, then thread it through the beads. Trim the string, leaving enough room at both ends to tie them together.

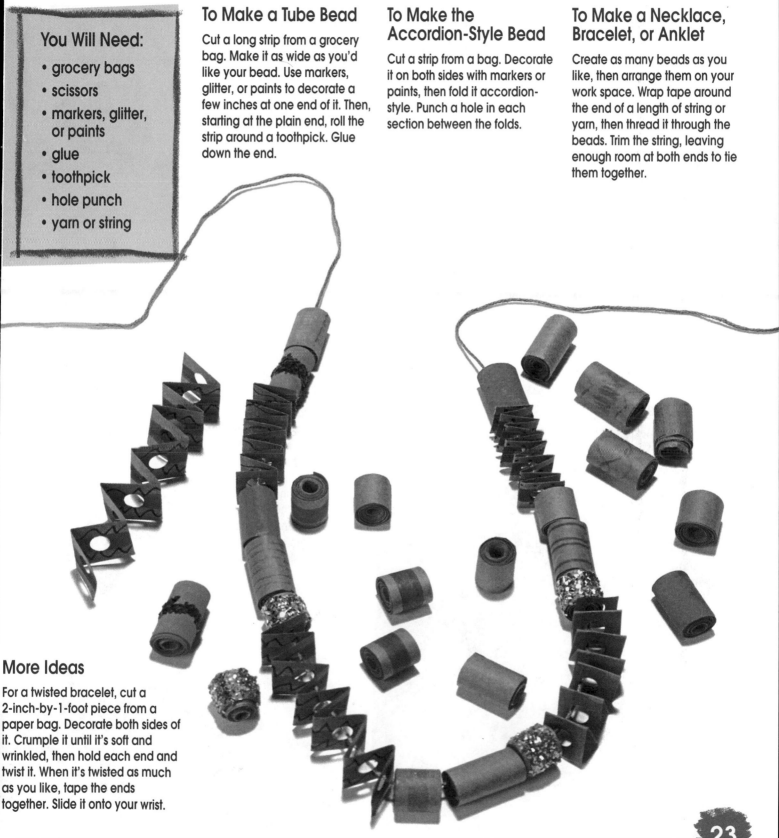

More Ideas

For a twisted bracelet, cut a 2-inch-by-1-foot piece from a paper bag. Decorate both sides of it. Crumple it until it's soft and wrinkled, then hold each end and twist it. When it's twisted as much as you like, tape the ends together. Slide it onto your wrist.

Barnyard Bag Games

Whether you're a city kid or a country child, you're sure to think these games are a hoot.

You Will Need:

- paper bags
- boxes
- gift-wrap tube
- scissors
- tape
- paints
- glue
- small rocks
- construction paper
- newspaper
- cylindrical container
- markers
- fabric
- dried beans
- rubber bands
- stapler
- plastic berry baskets
- cotton balls
- thin cardboard
- other accessories

To Make "Feed the Pig"

For the snout, cut off a short, tube-shaped section from a large cylindrical container. Trace around it onto a large box, and cut out the circle. Cut open a bag and use the paper to cover the box and the snout. Glue the snout into the hole in the box. Paint the pig. Glue on cut-paper ears and use markers to add eyes and feet. Curl a chenille stick, and glue it on the back as a tail.

For the feed, cut out three circles from fabric. Place dried beans in the center of each circle, then gather the edges and hold them with a rubber band. Try to toss the feed into the pig's mouth.

To Make "Bell the Cow"

On the top of a box, trace around the end of a gift-wrap tube. Cut out the hole. Wrap the box with paper. Cut a hole in the paper to match the hole in the box. Tape the paper in place, but leave one narrow side open. Paint the tube, and let it dry. Cut tabs in the bottom of the tube. Insert the tabbed end of the tube into the hole in the box, and glue the tabs against the opposite side. Let it dry. Fill the box with small rocks through the open side. Seal that side, then paint the box and let it dry.

Turn a white bag upside down, and paint it to look like a cow's head. Glue on cut-paper ears. Stuff some newspaper into the head, and tape it around the end of the tube.

To make each belled collar, cut down the seam of three lunch bags and cut off the bottom sections. Twist each long rectangular strip, then tape them together into a circle. (It should fit over the cow's head.) Paint the ring and let it dry. Tie on a large jingle bell. Try to toss the belled collar onto the cow.

To Make "Cornfield Bowling"

Use a pencil to draw an ear of corn on six lunch bags. Leave a few inches of blank space at the top of each bag. Paint the corn and let it dry. Outline the corn with a black marker. Stuff the bags with newspaper. Fold down the tops of the bags, and staple them closed.

To play, arrange the corn in a triangle, then use a rubber ball to bowl over as many as you can.

To Make "Hens and Chicks"

Game Board

Create a large triangular board out of bag paper. Paint the board, and let it dry. Use markers to draw spaces at least 2 inches long. Make the same number of spaces on each side of the triangle. From paper, create a short path with 3 spaces leading out from each side of the triangle. Leave space to glue the nests on the ends.

Spinner

Cut out a circle from cardboard and paint it, as shown. Add numbers from 1 to 4. Glue it in the middle of the game board, and let it dry. Cut an arrow out of cardboard and paint it. Poke a hole in the arrow, the spinner, and the game board. Fasten the arrow loosely to the board with a metal fastener.

Nests

Cut a few inches from the top of a lunch bag, then fringe the sides and curl the ends around a pencil. Glue the nests onto the ends of the paths leading out from the board.

Chicks

Dip cotton balls in paint and let them dry. Make four red chicks, four brown chicks, and four yellow chicks. Glue on paper beaks and feet, and use a marker to add eyes. Place the matching chicks in the nests.

Hen Baskets

Cut a hen shape from the side of a paper bag and paint it. Paint one red hen, one brown hen, and one yellow hen. Glue each hen in a plastic berry basket. Poke a hole in each corner of the board, and tie on the hen baskets. Tie the red hen directly across from the nest with the red chicks, and the other hens across from the matching chicks.

How to Play

Three players are needed. The point of the game is to move your chicks from the nest to the matching hen. Each player takes a turn with the spinner. You are allowed to move one chick per spin, and you can move to the left or the right around the board. You can have all of your chicks on the board at once, if you wish. If you land on a space with a chick already on it, send the chick that was there back to the nest to start over. Whoever is the first player to move all of his or her chicks safely to the hen basket wins.

Coiled Baskets

With only a few materials and some patience, you can create a sturdy, attractive coiled basket.

You Will Need:

- grocery bags
- scissors
- ruler
- large-eye needle
- strong thread, string, or twine

1 Cut down one seam of a bag and cut off the bottom section. Cut the rectangular piece into long 3-inch-wide strips. Twist each strip into a tight rope.

2 Thread the needle. Form a small loop at the end of one twisted-paper rope. Wind the thread end (opposite the needle) six or seven times around the rope to hold the loop in place. Coil the rope once around the loop.

3 Pass the needle through the center of the loop, from top to bottom, to hold the coil. Make another stitch through the loop about a half-inch from the first. Make more stitches all the way around until you have a complete coil.

4 When you begin the next coil (and all the others), pierce the needle through the preceding coil every half-inch or inch to make a stitch. Add twisted-paper ropes when you need them by inserting them under the end of the coiled rope. Make the basket as large as you wish.

5 To finish the basket, knot the thread, then trim the rope end.

More Ideas

Decorate your basket with paints or markers, if you wish.

Use it as a fruit basket or a candy dish.

Gingerbread Men

These friendly fellows make any scene festive. String them over doorways or around a tree.

You Will Need:

- grocery bag
- scissors
- pencil
- paints

1 Cut a long strip from the bag. Fold it accordion-style. On the top section, draw a gingerbread man with the hands and feet touching the folds.

2 With the paper folded, cut out the man, but do not cut through the folded paper at the hands and feet.

3 Unfold the paper. The gingerbread men should be in a row, with hands and feet touching. Paint them.

More Ideas

Create other strings of things, such as kissing fish, leaping dolphins, a fleet of jets, or a line of ducklings.

Paper-Bag Snowman

This smiling snowman can sit inside all winter without melting.

You Will Need:

- paper bags
- newspaper
- rubber band
- pencil
- tape
- scissors
- construction paper
- glue
- cylindrical snack container
- twigs
- felt

1 For the body, stuff a large bag with newspaper. Gather the bag at the opening and secure it with a rubber band.

2 For the head, stuff a small bag with newspaper. Stick one end of a pencil in the opening. Gather the bag around the pencil and secure it with tape to form a neck. The other end of the pencil should be sticking out. Stretch open the rubber band on the body, and insert the neck in the opening.

3 For a hat brim, cut out a paper circle, and glue it on the head. Cut off one end of the snack container, glue paper onto it, and glue it on the brim. For arms, stick a twig into each side of the body. Add a felt scarf, a hatband, and paper details.

More Ideas

Make other characters, such as Uncle Sam or a favorite story character.

Mask Mania!

Invent all kinds of masks—funny ones, scary ones, animals, or other creatures.

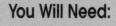

You Will Need:

- grocery bags
- scissors
- ribbon
- pencil
- markers
- paints
- construction paper
- glue

To Make the Ponytailed Lady

Cut out the bottom of a bag. Cut fringe around the top, gather it, and tie it with ribbon. Ask an adult to curl the ribbon with scissors. Use this bag and follow step 1 under "To Make the Square Masks." Add details with markers.

To Make the Square Masks

1 Put a bag over your head. Place your fingers where your mouth and eyes are. Remove the bag from your head, leaving your fingers there. Draw eyes and a mouth. Cut them out.

2 Trim a few inches from the opening of the bag, or cut curved slots in the sides so the mask can rest on your shoulders.

3 Follow the instructions for the mask you want to make.

To Make the Clown

Paint eyes, eyebrows, a nose, and a mouth on the front of the bag. Make a bow tie and a hat from construction paper, and glue them on. For hair, cut wide fringe in construction paper, and glue it on. Curl the ends around a pencil.

28

It's fun and easy to do, using large paper bags and a few other supplies.

To Make the Frog

Glue blue construction paper on the front of the bag. Cut out the paper eyeholes where they're already cut out of the bag. Cut out a frog, fly, and lily pad from paper and glue them on. Position the frog so that its eyes are above the top of the bag, and so that your eyeholes are the frog's nostrils.

To Make the Chick

Cut out eyes and a beak from construction paper. Add details with markers. Glue them on the front of the mask. For the feathers, cut out strips of paper. Glue them on the mask, and curl the ends around a pencil.

To Make the Bearded Man

Draw facial features and glasses with a marker. Cut out ears from a paper bag, and glue them on. For the beard, cut wide fringe in paper, and glue it on. Curl the ends around a pencil.

More Ideas

Before Halloween, have a mask-making party where all of the guests invent their own paper-bag masks.

For variety in your masks, use different materials, such as fake fur, feathers, chenille sticks, and scrap fabric. Some different masks to try making are elves, bears, cats, goblins, dogs, ghosts, and lions.

29

Fish Out of Water

These adorable fish are fun to make—and quick! Make a whole school of them.

You Will Need:

- paper bags
- glue
- newspaper
- rubber bands
- paints
- markers
- scissors
- construction paper

1 To form the nose, fold back and glue the two corners at the bottom of a closed bag. Stuff the bag with newspaper. A few inches from the open end, gather and hold it closed with a rubber band. For the tail, fan out the ends.

2 Paint the fish and decorate it with markers. Cut out fins from construction paper, and glue them on. Set your fish on a shelf as a decoration or attach a string and hang it up.

More Ideas

Make fish and other creatures, and have a party with an underwater theme.

Create a mobile by hanging small fish from a dowel.

Bright Yellow Duck

This duck doesn't swim, but it's still lots of fun.

You Will Need:

- white bag
- yellow paint
- newspaper
- string
- masking tape
- scissors
- construction paper
- glue
- markers

1 Paint the bag and let it dry. Fill it halfway with newspaper. Gather and tie it with a string above the filled part. Fill the rest of the bag with newspaper. Tape it closed.

2 Cut out wings, feet, eyes, feathers, and a beak from paper. Glue them on. Add details with markers.

More Ideas

Use the duck as a favor and place card for a party. Write the guest's name on the front. Fill it with peanuts (with the shells on), other treats, and small toys.

spooky Halloween Crafts

Ghosts suspended in midair, pumpkins grinning without care, a house with ghouls in every nook—you've found the scariest crafts in the book!

You Will Need:

- grocery bags
- foil
- scissors
- yarn
- stapler
- white bags
- glue
- markers
- clear fishing line
- flashlight

To Make the Trick-or-Treat Bag

Fold over the top of a bag several times to make a cuff. Cut a jack-o'-lantern from foil and glue it on the bag. For the handle, braid three bunches of yarn strands and knot each end. Tie the handle ends to the sides of the bag.

To Make the Floating Ghost

Cut out two arms from white paper. Glue them to the sides of a white bag. Use markers to draw a face on the front of the bag. Stuff the bag with newspaper, and staple it closed. Tie on clear fishing line as an "invisible" hanger.

To Make the Haunted House

On the front of a bag, use markers to draw and color a house. Cut out windows and doors. Place a flashlight inside the bag to create an eerie glow.

More Ideas

For a jack-o'-lantern centerpiece, stuff a paper bag with newspaper, tie the top with yarn, and decorate it.

Design a Doll

"Paper doll" takes on a whole new meaning with this classy trio.

You Will Need:

- grocery bags
- scissors
- ruler
- cotton balls
- string and yarn
- markers
- chenille sticks
- cardboard tubes
- glue
- rubber band
- needle and thread
- paints
- pompon
- plastic cap

More Ideas

Make a whole family. When making children, use shorter tubes and make the heads and arms smaller.

To Make the Basic Doll

1 Crumple up a paper bag until it is a small ball. Uncrumple the bag and smooth it out. Do this again and again until the bag is very soft. For the head, cut a 5-inch square from the soft paper bag. Wrap cotton balls in the center of the square. Tie it with string to form a neck. Use markers to add facial features.

2 Roll a 6-inch-by-3-inch piece of the soft paper around a chenille stick to form the arms. Tie the ends with string. Place the neck over the center of the arms and tuck the neck into a tube. Cut two notches out of the tube to set the arms in.

3 At the bottom end of the tube, cut a slit in the front and the back to form two legs. Use markers to add shoes.

They may look complex, but they're surprisingly simple to make.

To Make the Red-Haired Doll

For the pleated skirt, cut a strip from the soft paper, and use a marker to add a stripe along one side. Make a fold every half-inch or so. Glue the skirt around the waist. For the blouse, cut out a rectangular piece from the soft paper. Cut a slit in the center for the neck. Decorate it with markers. Place it over the head, with one end in front and the other in back. Make a sash from the soft paper, add a stripe along the middle, and tie it around the doll's waist. For hair, tie yarn strands together and glue them on the head.

To Make the Sailor Doll

Paint the body and the arms. For a neckerchief, cut out a triangle from the soft paper and paint it. Glue it around the sailor's shoulders. For the hat, glue a pompon on a plastic cap and glue it on the head.

To Make the Black-Haired Doll

For the skirt, cut out a large circle from the soft paper. Decorate around the edge with a marker. Cut a hole in the middle and slide it onto the waist. Use a rubber band to hold it in place on the underside. Cut out a vest from the soft paper. Decorate around the edges with a marker and poke two holes in the sides for the arms. Put it on the doll. Punch a hole on each side in the front and tie string through them. For the shawl, cut a long strip from the soft paper and fold it over once. Cut fringe in the ends and drape it around the arms. For hair, tie yarn strands together and glue them on the head. For the hat, cut out a large circle from the soft paper. Ask an adult to help you sew a running stitch around the edge of the circle. Pull the thread ends to gather the hat, then tie them in a bow. Place the hat on the doll's head.

Costumes for Kids

Big, boxy paper bags are great for quick and clever costumes. Try making the ones below, or come up with your own costume ideas.

You Will Need:

- grocery bags
- scissors
- paints
- construction paper
- glue

1 Turn a bag upside down. Cut out a hole in the bottom section for your head. Or, to make a hole for your face, put a bag over your head. Place your hand on the bag where it covers your face. Remove the bag, leaving your hand there. Draw an oval shape at that spot. Cut out the oval.

2 Cut arm holes in the front of the bag or the sides. Or, cut off the sides of the bag completely. Paint the costume or cut out paper or fabric decorations and glue them on. Add other details, such as a paper lion's tail or paper-doily apron.

3 Create any props that you'll need, such as a shield.

More Ideas

Try these other costumes: a robot, a star, a box of your favorite cereal, or a bookworm (decorate the bag as the book, and yourself as the worm).

Brown-Bag Scrapbook

The heavyweight paper from a grocery bag is the perfect material to use for a lasting scrapbook.

You Will Need:
- grocery bags
- scissors
- yarn
- old magazines
- glue
- markers

1 Cut the large sides off of several grocery bags. Place the sheets on top of one another and fold the stack in half to make a book.

2 Open the book to the middle and poke two holes in the fold. String yarn through the holes and tie the ends together.

3 Cut letters from a magazine to spell the words "My Scrapbook." Glue them on the cover. Decorate with markers.

More Ideas
Create a calendar using seven large sheets. Turn the book sideways so the yarn is at the top. Create a drawing and a calendar grid on each spread.

Easy Book Covers

Give your books a personalized look while protecting them from wear and tear.

You Will Need:
- grocery bags
- scissors
- hardback book
- pencil
- markers

1 Cut down the seam of a bag, then cut off the bottom to form one long rectangle of paper. Position it horizontally in front of you.

2 Place a book in the center of the paper. Trace along the top and bottom of it onto paper. Remove the book. Fold along each line.

3 Place the book in the center of the paper again. Fold over each side of the paper to form flaps. If you wish, insert the book cover into the flaps. Decorate with markers.

More Ideas
Decorate your book covers with school symbols or colors, cut-paper decorations, ribbon, or fancy writing.

Village Scene

Create this colorful town using paper bags, paints, and cutouts from magazines.

You Will Need:

- paper bags
- pencil
- paints
- glue
- stapler
- old magazines
- scissors
- thin cardboard
- tape

To Make the Buildings

1 Lay a bag flat on your work surface. Leaving the top few inches blank, use a pencil to draw a building. Add details, such as a roof, shrubs, steps, windows, curtains, and a door.

2 Paint the design and let it dry. Open the bag, then close the top and fold it back three times. Staple or glue it closed. Position the building so it stands upright.

3 Make various kinds of buildings for your village, such as houses, apartment buildings, a grocery store, a barbershop, and a variety store.

Invent a town of your own, or model your scene on a place you've visited.

To Make the Cutouts

1 From old magazines, cut out pictures of people, cars, trees, and other objects for your paper-bag village.

2 Glue the cutout pictures onto thin cardboard, then cut around them.

3 To make a stand for each figure, cut out a triangular piece of cardboard that is slightly smaller than the figure, and tape it on the back.

More Ideas

Make a model of the area where you live. Draw the buildings near you, and add streets, bridges, and other landmarks. For people cutouts, use a mix of photos cut from old magazines and photos of your family and friends.

Look at postcards for ideas of other cities and towns that you can make.

Wise Old Owl

Whooo can make this owl in no time flat? Youuu can!

You Will Need:

- paper bags
- newspaper
- stapler
- glue
- scissors
- markers

1 Fill a bag halfway with newspaper. Close the bag, fold the top down twice, and staple it. Glue the stapled part down so it is as flat as the bottom of the bag. This will be the bottom of the owl.

2 From another bag, cut out feet, a face, wings, and feathers. Glue them on the owl. Add details with markers.

More Ideas

Use smaller paper bags to make baby owls.

Make other birds, such as a penguin, a puffin, a toucan, or a parrot.

Big Pink Bunny

This cheerful rabbit will brighten up any room.

You Will Need:

- paper bags
- pink paint
- newspaper
- ribbon
- scissors
- construction paper
- markers
- glue
- ice-cream sticks
- pompon
- cotton ball

1 Paint two bags and let them dry. Fill one bag with newspaper. Carefully pull the other bag over the top of the filled bag. Tie a ribbon around the bags for the rabbit's neck.

2 Cut out feet, eyes, and ears from construction paper. Add details with markers, and glue them on. Glue an ice-cream stick behind each ear for support. Draw whiskers and a mouth with markers, then glue on a pompon as a nose and a cotton ball as a tail.

More Ideas

Instead of stuffing the bunny with newspaper, fill him with a mixture of tissue paper and treats, such as wrapped candies or sandwich bags filled with cookies. Give the bunny as an Easter gift, along with a note with instructions to remove the top bag and look inside.

King-Size Octopus

It's hard to resist smiling back at these big friendly creatures.

You Will Need:

- grocery bags
- paints
- newspaper
- stapler
- glue
- ruler
- chenille sticks
- construction paper
- scissors

1 For the body, paint a grocery bag and let it dry. Stuff it with newspaper. Fold and staple the opening closed. Glue it in place so it is as flat as the bottom of the bag. Add cut-paper features for the face and glue them on.

2 For the legs or tentacles, cut down one side of a grocery bag and cut off the bottom section. Cut the large rectangle into long 5-inch-wide strips. Twist chenille sticks together, end to end, as long as each strip. Glue each paper strip around connected chenille sticks. Make eight legs. Paint them. Staple them onto the octopus's body and bend them to shape.

More Ideas

Make a jellyfish by gluing on wavy strips of tissue paper instead of legs.

Make a paper-bag caterpillar by stuffing a long bread bag with newspaper and gluing on short paper legs with chenille sticks in them.

Wrap It Up!

Why buy gift wrap when you can create your own? There are countless ways to decorate it.

You Will Need:

- grocery bags
- scissors
- newspaper
- sponge
- paints
- paintbrush
- large-eye needle
- ribbon
- glue
- paper plates
- tape

1 Cut down the seam of a bag, and cut off the bottom section. Use the large rectangle that's left. If you want a larger piece of gift wrap, tape together the paper from several bags.

2 Cover your work space with newspaper. Follow the instructions to decorate the gift wrap of your choice.

3 Wrap a gift with the paper, and add a bow or other trim on top of it.

Use handprinting, sponge-painting, or ribbon-weaving, then make bows for on top.

To Make the Sponge-Print Paper

Dip a small section of sponge in some paint, and dab it over the entire surface of the paper. Let it dry. Use a paintbrush to add white dots.

To Make the Woven-Ribbon Paper

Thread a large-eye needle with ribbon. Weave it through the paper and glue down the ends. Glue wider ribbon between some of the woven ribbons.

To Make the Handprint Paper

Spread some paint on a paper plate. Press your hand in it, then press your hand all over the paper. Use several colors if you wish, but use a different paper plate for each color, and wash your hands in between colors. Let the paint dry before overlapping handprints.

To Make the Fringed Paper Bow

Cut fringe along one side of several rectangular strips of paper. Fold the strips into squares (with the fringe all facing the same way), and glue them in place. Put glue around the squares near the bottom, and glue them together in a cluster. To glue them on a package, cut tabs from the bottoms of the outside squares, and glue the tabs to the package. Curl the fringe around a pencil.

More Ideas

Decorate gift wrap by finger-painting it, tracing around cookie cutters, or painting animals or balloons on it.

To make a greeting card or a gift tag for on top, see "Cards from Bugs" on page 47.

Fruit-Filled Cornucopia

This horn of plenty makes a great autumn centerpiece. For other seasons, arrange the fruits in a basket or bowl.

You Will Need:

- paper bags
- pencil
- paints
- scissors
- markers
- masking tape
- plaster of paris
- chenille sticks
- glue
- acrylic paints

1 Roll down the top few inches of a paper bag. Twist the bag tightly from bottom to top. At the top edge, gently open out the bag to form a cone shape.

2 On the sides of a grocery bag, draw and paint leaf shapes. When the paint dries, cut them out and add details with markers. Place them in the cornucopia.

3 To make the fruit, crumple bag paper into a fruit shape. Wrap masking tape around the shape.

4 Tear paper into tiny pieces. With an adult's help, mix plaster of paris according to the directions on the package. Add the tiny pieces of paper. Apply this mixture around the fruit shape, and let it dry.

5 To add a stem, poke a hole in the dried fruit, insert a chenille stick, and add glue. Paint the fruit with acrylic paints. Let it dry.

More Ideas

Make other kitchen decorations, such as artificial rolls, pretzels, and muffins.

Don't Litter! Bag

Help keep your family's car clean by making a litter bag for it.

You Will Need:

- paper bag
- scissors
- construction paper
- glue
- hole punch
- yarn

1 To form a cuff, fold down the top of the bag twice.

2 Draw and cut out pictures from construction paper. Glue them on the bag.

3 On one side of the bag, fold a small piece of paper over the cuff. Punch two holes through the cuff and the paper. For a hanger, thread a loop of yarn through the holes.

More Ideas

Notice if any rooms in your house, such as a basement or a workshop, could use a litter bag. Create a few and decorate them to match those rooms.

Paper-Bag Pilgrims

This jolly couple would look terrific as a centerpiece on your Thanksgiving table.

You Will Need:

- lunch bags
- paints
- newspaper
- stapler
- construction paper
- scissors
- glue

1 For the bodies, paint two lunch bags and let them dry. Stuff them with newspaper, then staple the tops closed.

2 Create heads from construction paper and glue them on the bodies. Add cut-paper collars, arms, hands, feet, and other details.

More Ideas

Make decorations for other holidays, such as cupids, leprechauns, bunnies, or groundhogs.

Puppets Take the Stage

Throw together an entire puppet show with a few bags, some supplies, and your imagination.

You Will Need:

- lunch bags
- grocery bags
- paints
- markers
- felt
- scissors
- glue
- construction paper
- buttons
- yarn and string
- chenille sticks
- ribbon
- pompons
- other decorations

To Make the Rabbit Puppet

Lay a bag smooth side up. Use markers to draw a rabbit face and paws. Glue on a pompon nose. Cut out ears from another bag, and glue them on the back of the head. Cut a short, vertical slit in the bag behind each ear and glue a small paper loop on the back of each ear for your fingers. Glue on a cotton ball as a tail.

To Make the Bear Puppet

Draw and paint a bear on the large side of a grocery bag. The lower section of the bear should be wide enough to put your hand through. Let it dry, then cut it out. Add details with markers. Trace around the bear onto another bag section. Cut it out. Glue the two shapes together at the edges only. Leave the lower section open. When it's dry, stuff the bear's head with paper.

To Make the Woodland Creature Puppet

On the bottom section of a lunch bag, paint a face and let it dry. Add details with markers and glue on a pompon nose. Paint an oval on the bag below the head. Cut out ears, legs, and a tail from another bag. Paint details on them. Cut fringe in the tail and weave a chenille stick through it. Glue the ears, legs, and tail onto the bag. Glue an acorn between its paws.

To Make the King Puppet

Lay a bag smooth side up. Cut out a crown from gift wrap, and decorate it with ribbon and sequins. Glue it at the top of the bag. Below the crown, glue on wiggle eyes and a mustache cut from felt. Below the mustache, cut two holes in the front of the bag. (For arms, stick your fingers through the holes.) Cut out a cape from felt and decorate it with rickrack. Glue it to the bag in the back. Punch two holes in the front of the cape and use string to tie the front corners together.

To Make the Lady Puppet

Use markers to draw a face on the bottom section of a lunch bag. Draw her top lip on the bottom section and her lower lip on the bag beneath it, so you can move her mouth. Use markers to draw her blouse. Cut a paper doily to make a lace collar. Glue it on. For a bow, poke two holes near the collar and tie a ribbon through them. Glue on a few buttons. For hair, poke holes along the top of her head and tie pieces of yarn through them.

To Make the Elf Puppet

Glue cut-paper eyes on the bottom section of a lunch bag. Cut out a hat from construction paper, and glue it above the eyes. Tie a jingle bell on the end of the hat. Glue a cut-paper shirt on the bag below the head. Add details with glitter and markers. Blow up a balloon partway and knot it. Poke a hole below the eyes, and insert the balloon knot through it.

More Ideas

For any puppet where you're using your fingers as arms, you might wish to make its clothes to match gloves that you have, so that the arms will match the body. You can also do this for rabbit or donkey ears—poke two holes in the top of the puppet and stick your gloved fingers through them as ears.

Here are some more ideas for puppets: a frog that opens its mouth to catch flies, a singer who carries a microphone, and a snake with a forked tongue (that's really your finger with a paper V taped on it).

45

Spirit Pennant

Make a pennant to show your support for a team, a club, or even your favorite person.

You Will Need:

- grocery bags
- scissors
- paints
- markers
- glue
- construction paper

1 Cut out a triangular shape from the large side of a paper grocery bag.

2 Paint it and let it dry. Use markers to add sayings and decorations.

3 Glue folded paper strips on the ends.

More Ideas

To decorate for a holiday or a party, string together a row of colorful pennants that spell out a saying. Put one letter on each pennant.

Handy Backpack

This whimsical backpack can hold a light lunch, some toy animal friends, or an extra sweater.

You Will Need:

- grocery bag
- scissors
- ruler
- paints
- fabric
- stapler

1 Fold the top of the bag down twice. On one large side, cut four 2-inch-wide slits: two near the top and two near the bottom. Paint the bag. Let it dry.

2 Pull a long strip of fabric through each set of slits. Staple the strips in place near the top of the backpack. Tie the strips to fit you.

More Ideas

Make a gift backpack by placing some tissue paper and a gift inside. Add a bow and a card. It's two gifts in one!

Cards from Bags

Turn those paper bags into thoughtful, handmade greeting cards or festive, colorful gift tags. Mail them to friends and relatives, or tie them onto gifts for a personal touch.

You Will Need:

- paper bags
- scissors
- large-eye needle
- yarn and string
- paper
- glue and tape
- hole punch
- photo
- paints
- colored pencils
- markers

1 Fold a section cut from a paper bag into the size you want your greeting card or gift tag to be.

2 Follow the instructions for the card you want to make.

3 For cards, write a greeting on the inside. For tags, punch a hole in the corner and tie it to a package with a string.

To Make the Duck Card

With a pencil, draw a duck on the card. Thread a needle with yarn, and sew a running stitch around the duck. Tape down the yarn ends. Add details with markers or colored pencils.

To Make the Photo Card

On the front of the card, cut out a shape that is slightly smaller than the photo. Tape the photo behind the shape. Paint hearts around the photo. Add details with colored pencils.

To Make the Tree Card

Cut out two trees from different colored paper. Glue one on top of the other so they don't line up exactly. Punch holes in the tree. Cut out a pot from paper. Glue the tree, pot, and punched circles on the card.

To Make the Gift Tags

Press your thumb in some paint, then press it on the tag to make a print. Let it dry. Decorate it with markers.

More Ideas

Create invitations and announcements from paper bags.

Try making a pop-up card by gluing a folded section inside.

Title Index

Subject Index